ON THE
HOLY SPIRIT
- St. Gregory of Nyssa -

Copyright © 2014 Beloved Publishing

All rights reserved. No part of this book may be reproduced, scanned, or distributed in any printed or electronic form without permission.

Printed in the United States of America

ISBN:163174044x

Against the Followers of Macedonius.

It may indeed be undignified to give any answer at all to the statements that are foolish; we seem to be pointed that way by Solomon's wise advice, "not to answer a fool according to his folly." But there is a danger lest through our silence error may prevail over the truth, and so the rotting sore [1] of this heresy may invade it, and make havoc of the sound word of the faith. It has appeared to me, therefore, to be imperative to answer, not indeed according to the folly of these men who offer objections of such a description to our Religion, but for the correction of their depraved ideas. For that advice quoted above from the Proverbs gives, I think, the watchword not for silence, but for the correction of those who are displaying some act of folly; our answers, that is, are not to run on the level of their foolish conceptions, but rather to overturn those unthinking and deluded views as to doctrine.

What then is the charge they bring against us? They accuse us of profanity for entertaining lofty conceptions about the Holy Spirit. All that we, in following the teachings of the Fathers, confess as to the Spirit, they take in a sense of their own, and make it a handle against us, to denounce us for

---

[1] sepedonodes...gangraina: both used by Galen.

profanity[2]. We, for instance, confess that the Holy Spirit is of the same rank as the Father and the Son, so that there is no difference between them in anything, to be thought or named, that devotion can ascribe to a Divine nature. We confess that, save His being contemplated as with peculiar attributes in regard of Person, the Holy Spirit is indeed from God, and of the Christ, according to Scripture[3], but that, while not to be confounded with the Father in being never originated, nor with the Son in being the Only-begotten, and while to be regarded separately in certain distinctive properties, He has in all else, as I have just said, an exact identity[4] with them. But our opponents aver that He is a stranger to any vital communion with the Father and the Son; that by

---

[2] eis asebeian graphein. This is Mai's reading. Cf. asebeias graphe. The active (instead of middle) in this sense is found in Aristoph. Av. 1052: the passive is not infrequent in Demosthenes and AEschines.

[3] From God, and of the Christ, according to Scripture. This is noticeable. The Greek is ek tou Theou esti, kai tou Christou esti, kathos gegraptai. Compare the words below "proceeding from the Father, receiving from the Son."

[4] to aparallakton (but there is something lost before this: perhaps to henomenon). This word is used to express substantial identity. Origen uses it in alluding to the "Stoic resurrection," i.e. the time when the "Great Year" shall again begin, and the world's history be literally repeated, i.e. the "identical Socrates shall marry the identical Xantippe, and teach the identical philosophy, &c." This expression was a favourite one also with Chrysostom and Cyril of Alexandria to express the identity of Glory, of Godhead, and of Honour, in the Blessed Trinity.

reason of an essential variation He is inferior to, and less than they in every point; in power, in glory, in dignity, in fine in everything that in word or thought we ascribe to Deity; that, in consequence, in their glory He has no share, to equal honour with them He has no claim; and that, as for power, He possesses only so much of it as is sufficient for the partial activities assigned to Him; that with the creative force He is quite disconnected.

Such is the conception of Him that possesses them; and the logical consequence of it is that the Spirit has in Himself none of those marks which our devotion, in word or thought, ascribes to a Divine nature. What then, shall be our way of arguing? We shall answer nothing new, nothing of our own invention, though they challenge us to it; we shall fall back upon the testimony in Holy Scripture about the Spirit, whence we learn that the Holy Spirit is Divine, and is to be called so. Now, if they allow this, and will not contradict the words of inspiration, then they, with all their eagerness to fight with us, must tell us why they are for contending with us, instead of with Scripture. We say nothing different from that which Scripture says.–But in a Divine nature, as such, when once we have believed in it, we can recognize no distinctions suggested either by the Scripture teaching or by our own common sense; distinctions, that is, that would divide that Divine and transcendent nature within itself by any degrees of intensity and remission, so as to be altered from itself by being more or less. Because we firmly believe that it is simple, uniform, incomposite, because we see in it no complicity or composition of dissimilars, therefore it is that, when once our minds have grasped the idea of Deity, we accept by the implication of that very name the perfection in it of every conceivable thing that befits the Deity. Deity, in fact, exhibits perfection in every line in which the good can be found. If it fails and comes short of perfection in any single point, in that point the conception of Deity will be impaired, so that it cannot, therein, be or be called Deity at all; for how could we apply that word to a thing that is imperfect and deficient, and requiring an addition external to itself?

We can confirm our argument by material instances. Fire naturally imparts the sense of heat to those who touch it, with all its component parts[5]; one part of it does not have the heat more intense, the other less intense; but as long as it is fire at all, it exhibits an invariable oneness with itself in an absolutely complete sameness of activity; if in any part it gets cooled at all, in that part it can no longer be called fire; for, with the change of its heat-giving activity into the reverse, its name also is changed. It is the same with water, with air, with every element that underlies the universe; there is one and the same description of the element, in each case, admitting of

---

[5] Reading moriois (cf. the same word below) for morian.

no ideas of excess or defect; water, for instance, cannot be called more or less water; as long as it maintains an equal standard of wetness, so long the term water will be realized by it; but when once it is changed in the direction of the opposite quality[6] the name to be applied to it must be changed also. The yielding, buoyant, "nimble"[7] nature of the air, too, is to be seen in every part of it; while what is dense, heavy, downward gravitating, sinks out of the connotation of the very term "air." So Deity, as long as it possesses perfection throughout all the properties that devotion[8] may attach to it, by virtue of this perfection in everything good does not belie its name; but if any one of those things that contribute to this idea of perfection is subtracted from it, the name of Deity is falsified in that particular, and does not apply to the subject any longer. It is equally impossible to apply to a dry substance the name of water, to that whose quality is a state of coolness the name of fire, to stiff and hard things the name of air, and to call that thing Divine which does not at once imply the idea of perfection; or rather the impossibility is greater in this last case.

If, then, the Holy Spirit is truly, and not in name only, called Divine both by Scripture and by our Fathers, what ground is left for those who oppose the

---

[6] pros ten enantian poioteta.
[7] nimble, kouphon; compare Macbeth, I. vi. "The air Nimbly and sweetly recommends itself Unto our senses."
[8] Reading eusebos.

glory of the Spirit? He is Divine, and absolutely good, and Omnipotent, and wise, and glorious, and eternal; He is everything of this kind that can be named to raise our thoughts to the grandeur of His being. The singleness of the subject of these properties testifies that He does not possess them in a measure only, as if we could imagine that He was one thing in His very substance, but became another by the presence of the aforesaid qualities. That condition is peculiar[9] to those beings who have been given a composite nature; whereas the Holy Spirit is single and simple in every respect equally. This is allowed by all; the man who denies it does not exist. If, then, there is but one simple and single definition of His being, the good which He possesses is not an acquired good; but, whatever He may be besides, He is Himself Goodness, and Wisdom, and Power, and Sanctification, and Righteousness, and Everlastingness, and Imperishability, and every name that is lofty, and elevating above other names. What, then, is the state of mind that leads these men, who do not fear the fearful sentence passed upon the blasphemy against the Holy Ghost, to maintain that such a Being does not possess glory? For they clearly put that statement forward; that we ought not to believe that He should be glorified: though I know not for what reason they judge it to be expedient not to confess the true nature of that which is essentially glorious.

---

[9] Reading idion gar touto.

For the plea will not avail them in their self-defence, that He is delivered by our Lord to His disciples third in order, and that therefore He is estranged from our ideal of Deity. Where in each case activity in working good shows no diminution or variation whatever, how unreasonable it is to suppose the numerical order to be a sign of any diminution or essential variation[10]! It is as if a man were to see a separate flame burning on three torches (and we will suppose that the third flame is caused by that of the first being transmitted to the middle, and then kindling the end torch[11]), and were to maintain that the heat in the first exceeded that of the others; that that next it showed a variation from it in the direction of the less; and that the third could not be called fire at all, though it burnt and shone just like fire, and did everything that fire does. But if there is really no hindrance to the third torch being fire, though it has been kindled from a previous flame, what is the philosophy of these men, who profanely think that they can slight the dignity of the Holy Spirit because He is named by the Divine lips after

---

[10] Reading elattoseos tinos e kata phusin parallages, k. t. l.
[11] The Ancient Greek Fathers, speaking of this procession, mention the Father only, and never, I think, express the Son, as sticking constantly in this to the language of the Scriptures (John xv. 26)"–Pearson. The language of the above simile of Gregory would be an illustration of this. So Greg. Naz., Orat. I. de Filio, "standing on our definitions, we introduce the Ungenerate, the Generated, and that which proceeds from the Father." This last expression was so known and public, that it is recorded even by Lucian in his Philopatris, S:12.

the Father and the Son? Certainly, if there is in our conceptions of the Substance of the Spirit anything that falls short of the Divine ideal, they do well in testifying to His not possessing glory; but if the highness of His dignity is to be perceived in every point, why do they grudge to make the confession of His glory? As if any one after describing some one as a man, were to consider it not safe to go on to say of him as well that he is reasoning, mortal, or anything else that can be predicated of a man, and so were to cancel what he had just allowed; for if he is not reasoning, he is not a man at all; but if the latter is granted, how can there be any hesitation about the conceptions already implied in "man"? So, with regard to the Spirit, if when one calls Him Divine one speaks the truth, neither when one defines Him to be worthy of honour, to be glorious, good, omnipotent, does one lie; for all such conceptions are at once admitted with the idea of Deity. So that they must accept one of two alternatives; either not to call Him Divine at all, or to refrain from subtracting from His Deity any one of those conceptions which are attributable to Deity. We must then, most surely, comprehend along with each other these two thoughts, viz. the Divine nature, and along with it a just idea, a devout intuition[12], of that Divine and transcendent nature.

---

[12] Reading kai tes eusebous ennoias.

Since, then, it has been affirmed, and truly affirmed, that the Spirit is of the Divine Essence, and since in that one word "Divine" every idea of greatness, as we have said, is involved, it follows that he who grants that Divinity has potentially granted[13] all the rest;— the gloriousness, the omnipotence, everything indicative of superiority. It is indeed a monstrous thing to refuse to confess this in the case of the Spirit; monstrous, because of the incongruity, as applied to Him, of the terms which in the list of opposites correspond to the above terms. I mean, if one does not grant gloriousness, one must grant the absence of gloriousness; if one sets aside His power, one must acquiesce in its opposite. So also with regard to honour, and goodness, and any other superiority, if they are not accepted, their opposites must be conceded.

But if all must shrink from that, as going even beyond the most revolting blasphemy, then a devout mind must accept the nobler names and conceptions of the Holy Spirit, and must pronounce concerning Him all that we have already named, that He has honour, power, glory, goodness, and everything else that inspires devotion. It must own, too, that these realities do not attach to Him in imperfection or with any limit to the quality of their brilliance, but that they correspond with their names to infinity. He

---

[13] The edition of Cardinal Mai has ho ekeino dous te dunamei, sunomologese, k. t. l. But the sense requires the comma to be placed after dous.

is not to be regarded as possessing dignity up to a certain point, and then becoming different; but He is always such. If you begin to count behind the ages, or if you fix your gaze on the Hereafter[14], you will find no falling off whatever in dignity, or glory, or omnipotence, such as to constitute Him capable of increase by addition, or of diminution by subtraction. Being wholly and entirely perfect, He admits diminution in nothing. Whereinsoever, on such a supposition as theirs, He is lessened, therein He will be exposed to the inroad of ideas tending to dishonour Him. For that which is not absolutely perfect must be suspected on some one point of partaking of the opposite character. But if to entertain even the thought of this is a sign of extreme derangement of mind, it is well to confess our belief that His perfection in all that is good is altogether unlimited, uncircumscribed, in no particular diminished.

If such is the doctrine concerning Him when followed out[15], let the same inquiry be made concerning the Son and the Father as well. Do you not confess[16] a perfection of glory in the case of the one as in the case of the other? I think that all who reflect will allow it. If, then, the honour of the Father is perfect, and the honour of the Son is perfect, and they have confessed as well the perfection of honour

---

[14] Reading to ephexes.
[15] ephexes.
[16] Reading homologeis

for the Holy Spirit, wherefore do these new theorists dictate to us that we are not to allow in His case an equality of honour with the Father and the Son? As for ourselves, we follow out the above considerations and find ourselves unable to think, as well as to say, that that which requires no addition for its perfection is, as compared with something else, less dignified; for when we have something wherein, owing to its faultless perfection, reason can discover no possibility of increase, I do not see either wherein it can discover any possibility of diminution. But these men, in denying the equality of honour, really lay down the comparative absence of it; and so also when they follow out further this same line of thought, by a diminution arising from comparison they divert all the conceptions that devotion has formed of the Holy Spirit; they do not own His perfection either in goodness, or omnipotence, or in any such attribute. But if they shrink from such open profanity and allow His perfection in every attribute of good, then these clever people must tell us how one perfect thing can be more perfect or less perfect than another perfect thing; for so long as the definition of perfection applies to it, that thing can not admit of a greater and a less in the matter of perfection.

If, then, they agree that the Holy Spirit is perfect absolutely, and it has been admitted in addition that true reverence requires perfection in every good thing for the Father and the Son as well, what reasons can justify them in taking away the Father[17] when once they have granted Him? For to take away "equality of dignity" with the Father is a sure proof that they do not think that the Spirit has a share in the perfection of the Father. And as regards the idea itself of this honour in the case of the Divine Being, from which they would exclude the Spirit, what do they mean by it? Do they mean that honour which men confer on men, when by word and gesture they pay respect to them, signifying their own deference in the form of precedence and all such-like practices, which in the foolish fashion of the day are kept up in the name of "honour." But all these things depend on the goodwill of those who perform them; and if we suppose a case in which they do not choose to perform them, then there is no one amongst mankind who has from mere nature any advantage, such that he should necessarily be more honoured than the rest; for all are marked alike with the same natural proportions. The truth of this is clear; it does not admit of any doubt. We see, for instance, the man who to-day, because of the office which he holds, is considered by the crowd an object of honour, becoming tomorrow himself one of those

---

[17] i.e. from fellowship with the Spirit. The text is tis ho logos kath' hon eulogon krinousin patera anairein, dedokasi; (for which dedokosi is a conjecture). But perhaps pneuma anairein, didaskosi, or didaxosi, would be a more intelligible reading; though the examples of the hortatory subjunctive other than in the first person are, according to Porson (ad Eurip. Hec. 430), to be reckoned among solecisms in classical Greek.]

who pay honour, the office having been transferred to another. Do they, then, conceive of an honour such as that in the case of the Divine Being, so that, as long as we please to pay it, that Divine honour is retained, but when we cease to do so it ceases too at the dictate of our will? Absurd thought, and blasphemous as well! The Deity, being independent of us, does not grow in honour; He is evermore the same; He cannot pass into a better or a worse state; for He has no better, and admits no worse.

In what sort of manner, then, can you honour the Deity? How can you heighten the Highest? How can you give glory to that which is above all glory? How can you praise the Incomprehensible? If "all the nations are as a drop of a bucket[18]," as Isaiah says, if all living humanity were to send up one united note of praise in harmony together, what addition will this gift of a mere drop be to that which is glorious essentially? The heavens are telling the glory of God[19], and yet they are counted poor heralds of His worth; because His Majesty is exalted, not as far as the heavens, but high above those heavens, which are themselves included within a small fraction of the Deity called figuratively His "span[20]." And shall a man, this frail and short-lived creature, so aptly likened to "grass," who "to-day is," and to-morrow is not, believe that he can worthily honour the Divine

---

[18] Is. xl. 15. But Mai's text has stathmos, not stagon (LXX.).
[19] Ps. xix. 1.
[20] Is. xl. 12. Tis emetrjse…ton ouranon spithame.

Being? It would be like some one lighting a thin fibre from some tow and fancying that by that spark he was making an addition to the dazzling rays of the sun. By what words, pray, will you honour the Holy Spirit, supposing you do wish to honour Him at all? By saying that He is absolutely immortal, without turning, or variableness, always beautiful, always independent of ascription from others, working as He wills all things in all, Holy, leading, direct, just, of true utterance, "searching the deep things of God," "proceeding from the Father," "receiving[21] from the Son," and all such-like things, what, after all, do you lend to Him by these and such-like terms? Do you mention what He has, or do you honour Him by what He has not? Well, if you attest what He has not, your ascription is meaningless and comes to nothing; for he who calls bitterness "sweetness," while he lies himself, has failed to commend that which is blamable. Whereas, if you mention what He has, such and such a quality is essential, whether men recognize it or not; He remains the object of faith [22], says the Apostle, if we have not faith.

What means, then, this lowering and this expanding of their soul, on the part of these men who are enthusiastic for the Father's honour, and grant to the Son an equal share with Him, but in the case of the

---

[21] lambanomenon
[22] pistos. 2 Tim. ii. 13.

Spirit are for narrowing down their favours; seeing that it has been demonstrated that the intrinsic worth of the Divine Being does not depend for its contents upon any will of ours, but has been always inalienably inherent in Him? Their narrowness of mind, and unthankfulness, is exposed in this opinion of theirs, while the Holy Spirit is essentially honourable, glorious, almighty, and all that we can conceive of in the way of exaltation, in spite of them.

"Yes," replies one of them, "but we have been taught by Scripture that the Father is the Creator, and in the same way that it was through the Son[23] ' that all things were made'; but God's word tells us nothing of this kind about the Spirit; and how, then, can it be right to place the Holy Spirit in a position of equal dignity with One Who has displayed such magnificence of power through the Creation?"

What shall we answer to this? That the thoughts of their hearts are so much idle talk, when they imagine that the Spirit was not always with the Father and the Son, but that, as occasion varies, He is sometimes to be contemplated as alone, sometimes to be found in the closest union with Them. For if the heaven, and the earth, and all created things were really made through the Son and from the Father, but apart from the Spirit, what was the Holy Spirit doing at the time when the Father was at work with the Son

---

[23] S. John i. 3

upon the Creation? Was He employed upon some other works, and was this the reason that He had no hand in the building of the Universe? But, then, what special work of the Spirit have they to point to, at the time when the world was being made? Surely, it is senseless folly to conceive of a creation other than that which came into existence from the Father through the Son. Well, suppose that He was not employed at all, but dissociated Himself from the busy work of creating by reason of an inclination to ease and rest, which shrank from toil?

May the gracious Spirit Himself pardon this baseless supposition of ours! The blasphemy of these theorists, which we have had to follow out in every step it takes, has caused us unwittingly to soil our discussion with the mud of their own imaginings. The view which is consistent with all reverence is as follows. We are not to think of the Father as ever parted from the Son, nor to look for the Son as separate from the Holy Spirit. As it is impossible to mount to the Father, unless our thoughts are exalted thither through the Son, so it is impossible also to say that Jesus is Lord except by the Holy Spirit. Therefore, Father, Son, and Holy Spirit are to be known only in a perfect Trinity, in closest consequence and union with each other, before all creation, before all the ages, before anything whatever of which we can form an idea[24]. The Father

---

[24] pro pases kataleptes epinoias.

is always Father, and in Him the Son, and with the Son the Holy Spirit. If these Persons, then, are inseparate from each other, how great is the folly of these men who undertake to sunder this indivisibility by certain distinctions of time, and so far to divide the Inseparable as to assert confidently, "the Father alone, through the Son alone, made all things"; the Holy Spirit, that is, being not present at all on the occasion of this making, or else not working. Well, if He was not present, they must tell us where He was; and whether, while God embraces all things, they can imagine any separate standing-place for the Spirit, so that He could have remained in isolation during the time occupied by the process of creating. If, on the other hand, He was present, how was it that He was inactive? Because He could not, or because He would not, work? Did He abstain willingly, or because some strong necessity drove Him away? Now, if He deliberately embraced this inactivity, He must reject working in any other possible way either; and He Who affirmed that "He worketh all things in all, as He wills[25]," is according to them a liar. If, on the contrary, this Spirit has the impulse to work, but some overwhelming control hinders His design, they must tell us the wherefore of this hindrance. Was it owing to his being grudged a share in the glory of those operations, and in order to secure that the admiration at their success should not extend to a third person as its object; or to a

---

[25] 1 Cor. xiii. 6.

distrust of His help, as if His co-operation would result in present mischief? These clever men most certainly furnish the grounds for our holding one of these two hypotheses; or else, if a grudging spirit has no connection with the Deity, any more than a failure can be conceived of in any relation to an Infallible Being, what meaning of any kind is there in these narrow views of theirs, which isolate the Spirit's power from all world-building efficiency? Their duty rather was to expel their low human way of thinking, by means of loftier ideas, and to make a calculation more worthy of the sublimity of the objects in question. For neither did the Universal God make the universe "through the Son," as needing any help, nor does the Only-begotten God work all things "by the Holy Spirit," as having a power that comes short of His design; but the fountain of power is the Father, and the power of the Father is the Son, and the spirit of that power is the Holy Spirit; and Creation entirely, in all its visible and spiritual extent, is the finished work of that Divine power. And seeing that no toil can be thought of in the composition of anything connected with the Divine Being (for performance being bound to the moment of willing, the Plan at once becomes a Reality), we should be justified in calling all that Nature which came into existence by creation a movement of Will, an impulse of Design, a transmission of Power, beginning from the Father, advancing through the Son, and completed in the Holy Spirit.

This is the view we take, after the unprofessional way usual with us; and we reject all these elaborate sophistries of our adversaries, believing and confessing as we do, that in every deed and thought, whether in this world, or beyond this world, whether in time or in eternity, the Holy Spirit is to be apprehended as joined to the Father and Son, and is wanting in no wish or energy, or anything else that is implied in a devout conception of Supreme Goodness[26]; and, therefore, that, except for the distinction of order and Person, no variation in any point is to be apprehended; but we assert that while His place is counted third in mere sequence after the Father and Son, third in the order of the transmission, in all other respects we acknowledge His inseparable union with them; both in nature, in honour, in godhead, and glory, and majesty, and almighty power, and in all devout belief.

But with regard to service and worship, and the other things which they so nicely calculate about, and bring into prominence, we say this; that the Holy Spirit is exalted above all that we can do for Him with our merely human purpose; our worship is far beneath the honour due; and anything else that in human customs is held as honourable is somewhere below the dignity of the Spirit; for that which in its essence is measureless surpasses those

---

[26] kata to agathon; probably here in its Platonic, rather than its ordinary sense.

who offer their all with so slight and circumscribed and paltry a power of giving. This, then, we say to those of them who subscribe to the reverential conception of the Holy Spirit that He is Divine, and of the Divine nature. But if there is any of them who rejects this statement, and this idea involved in the very name of Divinity, and says that which, to the destruction of the Spirit's greatness, is in circulation amongst the many, namely, that He belongs, not to making, but to made, beings, that it is right to regard Him not as of a Divine, but as of a created nature, we answer to a proposition such as this, that we do not understand how we can count those who make it amongst the number of Christians at all. For just as it would not be possible to style the unformed embryo a human being, but only a potential one, assuming that it is completed so as to come forth to human birth, while as long as it is in this unformed state, it is something other than a human being; so our reason cannot recognize as a Christian one who has failed to receive, with regard to the entire mystery, the genuine form of our religion[27]. We can hear Jews believing in God, and our God too: even our Lord reminds[28] them in the Gospel that they recognize no other God than the Father of the Only-begotten, "of Whom ye say that he is your God." Are we, then, to call the Jews Christians because they too agree to worship the God Whom we adore? I am

---

[27] ten alethe morphosin tes eusebeias
[28] entithetai: suntithetai, "concedes to," would perhaps be better.

aware, too, that the Manichees go about vaunting the name of Christ. Because they hold revered the Name to which we bow the knee, shall we therefore number them amongst Christians? So, too, he who both believes in the Father and receives the Son, but sets aside the Majesty of the Spirit, has "denied the faith, and is worse than an infidel," and belies the name of Christ which he bears. The Apostle bids the man of God to be "perfec[29]." Now, to take only the general man, perfection must consist in completeness in every aspect of human nature, in having reason, capability of thought and knowledge, a share of animal life, an upright bearing, risibility, broadness of nail; and if any one were to term some individual a man, and yet were unable to produce evidence in his case of the foregoing signs of human nature, his terming him so would be a valueless honour. Thus, too, the Christian is marked by his Belief in Father, Son, and Holy Ghost; in this consists the form of him who is fashioned [30] in accordance with the mystery of the truth. But if his form is arranged otherwise, I will not recognize the existence of anything whence the form is absent; there is a blurring out of the mark, and a loss of the essential form, and an alteration of the characteristic signs of our complete humanity, when the Holy Spirit is not included in the Belief. For indeed the word of

---

[29] t2 Cor. xiii. 11. Cf. 1 Cor. xiv. 20.
[30] Cf. 2 Tim. i. 13 (hupotuposin); Rom. ii. 20 (morphosin); vi. 17 (tupon), all referring to truth as contained in a formula. Cf. also Gal. iv. 19.

Ecclesiastes says true; your heretic is no living man, but "bones," he says[31], "in the womb of her that is with child [32]"; for how can one who does not think of the unction along with the Anointed be said to believe in the Anointed? "Him," says (Peter), "did God anoint with the Holy Spirit [33]."

These destroyers of the Spirit's glory, who relegate Him to a subject world, must tell us of what thing that unction is the symbol. It not a symbol of the Kingship? And what? Do they not believe in the Only-begotten as in His very nature a King? Men who have not once for all enveloped their hearts with the Jewish "vail[34]" will not gainsay that He is this. If, then, the Son is in His very nature a king, and the unction is the symbol of His kingship, what, in the way of a consequence, does your reason demonstrate? Why, that the Unction is not a thing alien to that Kingship, and so that the Spirit is not to be ranked in the Trinity as anything strange and foreign either. For the Son is King, and His living, realized, and personified Kingship is found in the Holy Spirit, Who anoints the Only-begotten, and so makes Him the Anointed, and the King of all things that exist. If, then, the Father is King, and the Only-begotten is King, and the Holy Ghost is the

---

[31] Reading kathos ekeinos phesin.
[32] Eccles. xi. 5 (LXX.). ouk esti ginoskon tis he hodos tou pneumatos, hos osta en gastri kuophorouses
[33] Acts x. 38. Cf. iv. 27.
[34] 2 Cor. iii. 14, 15.

Kingship, one and the same definition of Kingship must prevail throughout this Trinity, and the thought of "unction" conveys the hidden meaning that there is no interval of separation between the Son and the Holy Spirit. For as between the body's surface and the liquid of the oil nothing intervening can be detected, either in reason or in perception, so inseparable is the union of the Spirit with the Son; and the result is that whosoever is to touch the Son by faith must needs first encounter the oil in the very act of touching; there is not a part of Him devoid of the Holy Spirit. Therefore belief in the Lordship of the Son arises in those who entertain it, by means of the Holy Ghost; on all sides the Holy Ghost is met by those who by faith approach the Son. If, then, the Son is essentially a King, and the Holy Spirit is that dignity of Kingship which anoints the Son, what deprivation of this Kingship, in its essence and comparing it with itself, can be imagined?

Again, let us look at it in this way. Kingship is most assuredly shown in the rule over subjects. Now what is "subject" to this Kingly Being? The Word includes the ages certainly, and all that is in them; "Thy Kingdom," it says, "is a Kingdom of ages," and, by ages, it means every substance in them created in infinite space[35], whether visible or invisible; for in them all things were created by the Maker of those

---

[35] ek tou periechontos. This expression of Anaxagoras is repeated more than once in the Treatise "On the Soul."

ages. If, then, the Kingship must always be thought of along with the King, and the world of subjects is acknowledged to be something other than the world of rulers, what absurdity it is for these men to contradict themselves thus, attributing as they do the unction as an expression for the worth of Him Whose very nature it is to be a King, yet degrading that unction Itself to the rank of a subject, as if wanting in such worth! If It is a subject by virtue of its nature, then why is It made the unction of Kingship, and so associated with the Kingly dignity of the Only-begotten? If, on the other hand, the capacity to rule is shown by Its being included in the majesty of Kingship, where is the necessity of having everything dragged down to a plebeian[36] and servile lower condition, and numbered with the subject creation? When we affirm of the Spirit the two conditions, we cannot be in both cases speaking the truth: i.e. that He is ruling, and that He is subject. If He rules, He is not under any lord, but if He is subject, then He cannot be comprehended with the Being who is a King. Men are recognized as amongst men, angels amongst angels, everything amongst its kind; and so the Holy Spirit must needs be believed to belong to one only of two worlds; to the ruling, or to the inferior world; for between these two our reason can recognize nothing; no new invention of

---

[36] idiotiken. On 1 Cor. xiv. 16, O anapleron ton topon tou idiotou, Theodoret says, "idioten kalei ton en to laiko tagmati tetagmenon." Theophylact also renders the word by the same equivalent.

any natural attribute on the borderland of the Created and the Uncreated can be thought of, such as would participate in both, yet be neither entirely; we cannot imagine such an amalgamation and welding together of opposites by anything being blended of the Created and the Uncreated, and two opposites thus coalescing into one person, in which case the result of that strange mixture would not only be a composite thing, but composed of elements that were unlike, and disagreeing as to time; for that which receives its personality from a creation is assuredly posterior to that which subsists without a creation.

If, then, they declare the Holy Ghost to be blended of both, they must consequently view that blending as of a prior with a posterior thing; and, according to them, He will be prior to Himself; and reversely, posterior to Himself; from the Uncreated He will get the seniority, and from the Created the juniority. But, in the nature of things, this cannot be; and so it must most certainly be true to affirm of the Holy Spirit one only of these alternatives, and that is, the attribute of being Uncreated; for notice the amount of absurdity involved in the other alternative; all things that we can think of in the actual creation have, by virtue of all having received their existence by an act of creation, a rank and value perfectly equal in all cases, and so what reason can there be for separating the Holy Spirit from the rest of the creation, and ranking Him with the Father and the

Son? Logic, then, will discover this about Him; That which is contemplated as part of the Uncreated, does not exist by creation; or, if It does, then It has no more power than its kindred creation, It cannot associate itself with that Transcendent Nature; if, on the other hand, they declare that He is a created being, and at the same time has a power which is above the creation, then the creation will be found at variance with itself, divided into ruler and ruled, so that part of it is the benefactor, part the benefited, part the sanctifier, part the sanctified; and all that fund of blessings which we believe to be provided for the creation by the Holy Spirit are present in Him, welling up abundantly, and pouring forth upon others, while the creation remains in need of the thence-issuing help and grace, and receives, as a mere dole, those blessings which can be passed to it from a fellow-creature! That would be like favouritism and respecting of persons; when we know that there is no such partiality in the nature of things, as that those existences which differ in no way from each other on the score of substance should not have equal power; and I think that no one who reflects will admit such views. Either He imparts nothing to others, if He possesses nothing essentially; or, if we do believe that He does give, His possession beforehand of that gift must be granted; this capacity of giving blessings, whilst needing oneself no such extraneous help, is the peculiar and exquisite privilege of Deity, and of no other.

Then let us look to this too. In Holy Baptism, what is it that we secure thereby? Is it not a participation in a life no longer subject to death? I think that no one who can in any way be reckoned amongst Christians will deny that statement. What then? Is that life-giving power in the water itself which is employed to convey the grace of Baptism? Or is it not rather clear to every one that this element is only employed as a means in the external ministry, and of itself contributes nothing towards the sanctification, unless it be first transformed itself by the sanctification; and that what gives life to the baptized is the Spirit; as our Lord Himself says in respect to Him with His own lips, "It is the Spirit that giveth life;" but for the completion of this grace He alone, received by faith, does not give life, but belief in our Lord must precede, in order that the lively gift may come upon the believer, as our Lord has spoken, "He giveth life to whom He willeth." But further still, seeing that this grace administered through the Son is dependent on the Ungenerate Source of all, Scripture accordingly teaches us that belief in the Father Who engendereth all things is to come first; so that this life-giving grace should be completed, for those fit to receive it, after starting from that Source as from a spring pouring life abundantly, through the Only-begotten Who is the True life, by the operation of the Holy Spirit. If, then, life comes in baptism, and baptism receives its completion in the name of Father, Son, and Spirit, what do these men mean who count this Minister of life as nothing? If the gift is a slight one, they must tell us the thing that is more precious than this life. But if everything whatever that is precious is second to this life, I mean that higher and precious life in which the brute creation has no part, how can they dare to depreciate so great a favour, or rather the actual Being who grants the favour, and to degrade Him in their conceptions of Him to a subject world by disjoining Him from the higher world of deity[37]. Finally, if they will have it that this bestowal of life is a small thing, and that it means nothing great and awful in the nature of the Bestower, how is it they do not draw the conclusion which this very view makes inevitable, namely, that we must suppose, even with regard to the Only-begotten and the Father Himself, nothing great in Their life, the same as that which we have through the Holy Spirit, supplied as it is from the Father through the Son?

So that if these despisers and impugners of their very own life conceive of the gift as a little one, and decree accordingly to slight the Being who imparts the gift, let them be made aware that they cannot limit to one Person only their ingratitude, but must

---

[37] "Whether or not the Macedonians explicitly denied the Divinity of the Holy Ghost is uncertain; but they viewed Him as essentially separate from, and external to, the One Indivisible Godhead. The Nicene' Creed declares that He is the Lord, or Sovereign Spirit because the heretics considered Him to be a minister of God; and the Supreme Giver of Life, because they considered Him a mere instrument by which we receive the gift."–Newman's Arians, note p. 420.

extend its profanity beyond the Holy Spirit to the Holy Trinity Itself. For like as the grace flows down in an unbroken stream from the Father, through the Son and the Spirit, upon the persons worthy of it, so does this profanity return backward, and is transmitted from the Son to the God of all the world, passing from one to the other. If, when a man is slighted, He Who sent him is slighted (yet what a distance there was between the man and the Sender!), what criminality[38] is thereby implied in those who thus defy the Holy Spirit! Perhaps this is the blasphemy against our Law-giver[39] for which the judgment without remission has been decreed; since in Him the[40] entire Being, Blessed and Divine, is insulted also. As the devout worshipper of the Spirit sees in Him the glory of the Only-begotten, and in that sight beholds the image of the Infinite God, and by means of that image makes an outline, upon his own cognition[41], of the Original, so most plainly does this contemner[42] (of the Spirit), whenever he advances any of his bold statements against the glory of the Spirit, extend, by virtue of the same reasoning, his profanity to the Son, and beyond Him to the Father. Therefore, those who reflect must have fear

---

38 katakrisin
39 kata tou nomothetou is Mai's reading. But kata ton nomotheten, i.e. according to S. Mark iii. 29, S. Luke xii. 10, would be preferable. Migne reads para in this sense.
40 to has probably dropped out.
41 te gnosei heautou.
42 Something has dropped out here.

lest they perpetrate an audacity the result of which will be the complete blotting out of the perpetrator of it; and while they exalt the Spirit in the naming, they will even before the naming exalt Him in their thought, it being impossible that words can mount along with thought; still when one shall have reached the highest limit of human faculties, the utmost height and magnificence of idea to which the mind can ever attain, even then one must believe it is far below the glory that belongs to[43] Him, according to the words in the Psalms, that "after exalting the Lord our God, even then ye scarcely worship the footstool beneath His feet": and the cause of this dignity being so incomprehensible is nothing else than that He is holy.

If, then, every height of man's ability falls below the grandeur of the Spirit (for that is what the Word means in the metaphor of "footstool"), what vanity is theirs who think that there is within themselves a power so great that it rests with them to define the amount of value to be attributed to a being who is invaluable! And so they pronounce the Holy Spirit unworthy of some things which are associated with the idea of value, as if their own abilities could do far more than the Spirit, as estimated by them, is capable of. What pitiable, what wretched madness! They understand not what they are themselves when they talk like this, and what the Holy Spirit against

---

[43] epiballouses. Cf. Ps. xcix. 5; 2 Chron. xxviii. 2.

Whom they insolently range themselves. Who will tell these people that men are "a spirit that goeth forth and returneth not again[44]," built up in their mother's womb by means of a soiled conception, and returning all of them to a soiled earth; inheriting a life that is likened unto grass; blooming for a little during life's illusion[45], and then withering away, and all the bloom upon them being shed and vanishing; they themselves not knowing with certainty what they were before their birth, nor into what they will be changed, their soul being ignorant of her peculiar destiny as long as she tarries in the flesh? Such is man.

On the contrary the Holy Spirit is, to begin with, because of qualities that are essentially holy, that which the Father, essentially Holy, is; and such as the Only-begotten is, such is the Holy Spirit; then, again, He is so by virtue of life-giving, of imperishability, of unvariableness, of everlastingness, of justice, of wisdom, of rectitude, of sovereignty, of goodness, of power, of capacity to give all good things, and above them all life itself, and by being everywhere, being present in each, filling the earth, residing in the heavens, shed abroad upon supernatural Powers, filling all things according to the deserts of each, Himself remaining full, being with all who are worthy, and yet not parted from the

---

[44] Wisdom xvi. 14.
[45] biotikes apates.

Holy Trinity. He ever "searches the deep things of God," ever "receives" from the Son, ever is being "sent," and yet not separated, and being "glorified," and yet He has always had glory. It is plain, indeed, that one who gives glory to another must be found himself in the possession of superabundant glory; for how could one devoid of glory glorify another? Unless a thing be itself light, how can it display the gracious gift of light? So the power to glorify could never be displayed by one who was not himself glory[46], and honour, and majesty, and greatness. Now the Spirit does glorify the Father and the Son. Neither does He lie Who saith, "Them that glorify Me I glorify" [47]; and "I have glorified Thee [48]," is said by our Lord to the Father; and again He says, "Glorify Thou Me with the glory which I had with Thee before the world was[49]" The Divine Voice answers, "I have both glorified, and will glorify again[50]." You see the revolving circle of the glory moving from Like to Like. The Son is glorified by the Spirit; the Father is glorified by the Son; again the Son has His glory from the Father; and the Only-begotten thus becomes the glory of the Spirit. For with what shall the Father be glorified, but with the true glory of the Son: and with what again shall

---

[46] It is worth noticing that Gregory maintains (Hom. xv. on Canticles) that Doxa in Scripture means the Holy Ghost.
[47] Cf. 1 Sam. ii. 30.
[48] S. John xvii. 4
[49] S. John xvii. 5.
[50] S. John xii. 28

the Son be glorified, but with the majesty of the Spirit? In like manner, again, Faith completes the circle, and glorifies the Son by means of the Spirit, and the Father by means of the Son.

If such, then, is the greatness of the Spirit, and whatever is morally beautiful, whatever is good, coming from God as it does through the Son, is completed by the instrumentality of the Spirit that "worketh all in all," why do they set themselves against their own life? Why do they alienate themselves from the hope belonging to "such as are to be saved"? Why do they sever themselves from their cleaving unto God? For how can any man cleave unto the Lord unless the Spirit operates within us that union of ourselves with Him? Why do they haggle with us about the amount of service and of worship? Why do they use that word "worship" in an ironical sense, derogatory to a Divine and entirely Independent Being, supposing that they desire their own salvation? We would say to them, "Your supplication is the advantage of you who ask, and not the honouring of Him Who grants it. Why, then, do you approach your Benefactor as if you had something to give? Or rather, why do you refuse to name as a benefactor at all Him Who gives you your blessings, and slight the Life-giver while clinging to Life? Why, seeking for His sanctification, do you misconceive of the Dispenser of the Grace of sanctification; and as to the giving of those blessings, why, not denying that He has the power, do you deem Him not worthy to be asked to give, and fail to take this into consideration, viz. how much greater a thing it is to give some blessing than to be asked to give it? The asking does not unmistakably witness to greatness in him who is asked; for it is possible that one who does not have the thing to give might be asked for it, for the asking depends only on the will of the asker. But one who actually bestows some blessing has thereby given undoubted evidence of a power residing in him. Why then, while testifying to the greater thing in Him,—I mean the power to bestow everything that is morally beautiful[51]—do you deprive Him of the asking, as of something of importance; although his asking, as we have said, is often performed in the case of those who have nothing in their power, owing to the delusion of their devotees? For instance, the slaves of superstition ask the idols for the objects of their wishes; but the asking does not, in this instance of the idols, confer any glory; only people pay that attention to them owing to the deluded expectation that they will get some one of the things they ask for, and so they do not cease to ask. But you, persuaded as you are of what and how great things the Holy Spirit is the Giver, do you neglect the asking them from Him, taking refuge in the law which bids you worship God and serve Him only[52]?' Well, how will you worship Him only, tell me, when you have severed Him from

---

[51] kalon.
[52] Deut. vi. 13; x. 20.

His intimate union with His own Only-begotten and His own Spirit? This worship is simply Jewish.

But you will say, "When I think of the Father it is the Son (alone) that I have included as well in that term." But tell me; when you have grasped the notion of the Son have you not admitted therein that of the Holy Spirit too? For how can you confess the Son except by the Holy Spirit? At what moment, then, is the Spirit in a state of separation from the Son, so that when the Father is being worshipped, the worship of the Spirit is not included along with that of the Son? And as regards their worship itself, what in the world do they reckon it to be? They bestow it, as some exquisite piece of honour, upon the God over all, and convey it over, sometimes, so as to reach the Only-begotten also; but the Holy Spirit they regard as unworthy of such a privilege. Now, in the common parlance of mankind, that self-prostration of inferiors upon the ground which they practise when they salute their betters is termed worship. Thus, it was by such a posture that the patriarch Jacob, in his self-humiliation, seems to have wished to show his inferiority when coming to meet his brother and to appease his wrath; for "he bowed himself to the ground," says the Scripture, "three times"[53]; and Joseph's brethren, as long as they knew him not, and he pretended before them

---

[53] The LXX. has prosekunesen epi ten gen heptakis, Gen. xxxiii. 3.

that he knew them not, by reason of the exaltation of his rank reverenced his sovereignty with this worship; and even the great Abraham himself "bowed himself[54]" "to the children of Heth," a stranger amongst the natives of that land, showing, I opine, by that action, how far more powerful those natives were than sojourners. It is possible to speak of many such actions both in the ancient records, and from examples before our eyes in the world now [55].

Do they too, then, mean this by their worship? Well, is it anything but absurdity to think that it is wrong to honour the Holy Spirit with that with which the patriarch honoured even Canaanites? Or do they consider their "worship" something different to this, as if one sort were fitting for men, another sort for the Supreme Being? But then, how is it that they omit worship altogether in the instance of the Spirit, not even bestowing upon Him the worship conceded in the case of men? And what kind of worship do they imagine to be reserved especially for the Deity? Is it to be spoken word, or acted gesture? Well, but are not these marks of honour shared by men as well? In their case words are spoken and gestures acted. Is it not, then, plain to every one who possesses the least amount of reflection, that any gift worthy of the Deity mankind has not got to give; for the Author of

---

[54] prosekunese to lao tes ges, tois huiois tou Chet, Gen. xxiii. 7.

[55] tou biou. This is a late use of bios.

all blessings has no need of us. But it is we men who have transferred these indications of respect and admiration, which we adopt towards each other, when we would show by the acknowledgment of a neighbour's superiority that one of us is in a humbler position than another, to our attendance upon a Higher Power; out of our possessions we make a gift of what is most precious to a priceless Nature. Therefore, since men, approaching emperors and potentates for the objects which they wish in some way to obtain from those rulers, do not bring to them their mere petition only, but employ every possible means to induce them to feel pity and favour towards themselves, adopting a humble voice, and a kneeling position[56], clasping their knees, prostrating themselves on the ground, and putting forward to plead for their petition all sorts of pathetic signs, to wake that pity,—so it is that those who recognize the True Potentate, by Whom all things in existence are controlled, when they are

---

[56] Still the word proskunein became consecrated to the highest Christian worship while therapeuein was employed for address to the angels. "Every supplication, every prayer, every entreaty, and every giving of thanks must be offered to the Almighty through the High Priest who is over all the angels, the incarnate Word and God. And we shall make supplication and prayer to the Word Himself also, and we shall give Him thanks if we can distinguish prayer in its proper meaning from the wrong use of the word," Origen c. Cels. v. 4 (Cf. viii. 13, where he answers the question whether Gabriel, Michael, and the rest of the archangels should be addressed, therapeuesthai).

supplicating for that which they have at heart, some lowly in spirit because of pitiable conditions in this world, some with their thoughts lifted up because of their eternal mysterious hopes, seeing that they know not how to ask, and that their humanity is not capable of displaying any reverence that can reach to the grandeur of that Glory, carry the ceremonial used in the case of men into the service of the Deity. And this is what "worship" is,—that, I mean, which is offered for objects we have at heart along with supplication and humiliation. Therefore Daniel too bends the knees to the Lord, when asking His love for the captive people; and He Who "bare our sicknesses," and intercedes for us, is recorded in the Gospel to have fallen on His face, because of the man that He had taken upon Him, at the hour of prayer, and in this posture to have made His petition, enjoining thereby, I think, that at the time of our petition our voice is not to be bold, but that we are to assume the attitude of the wretched; since the Lord "resisteth the proud, but giveth grace unto the humble;" and somewhere else (He says), "he that exalteth himself shall be abased." If, then, "worship" is a sort of suppliant state, or pleading put forward for the object of the petition, what is the intention of these new-fashioned regulations? These men do not even deign to ask of the Giver, nor to kneel to the Ruler, nor to attend upon the Potentate.

Printed in Great Britain
by Amazon.co.uk, Ltd.,
Marston Gate.